Southampton

- Port with double tides
- Portal to the United Kingdom
- Gateway to the world

Southampton

We Saxons were attacked [by] the Vikings so we moved t[o] the high ground at Hamtun[.]

We Normans thought this would be a good spot for our walled town.

Hamtun

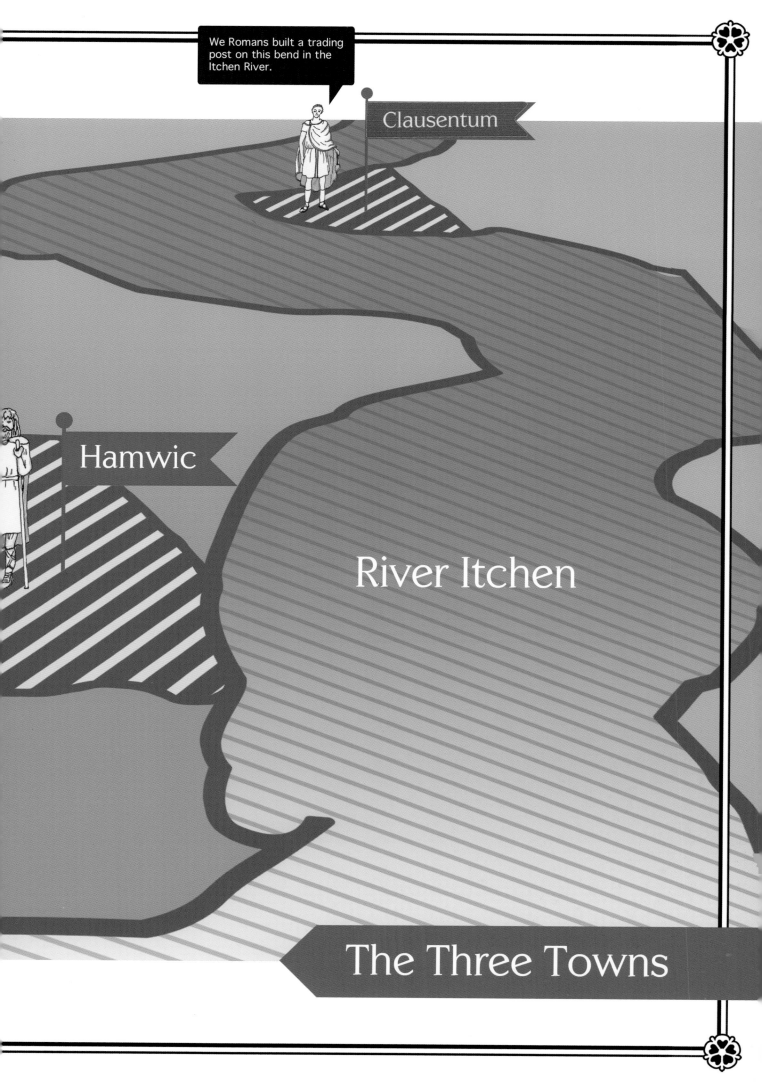

The Bargate has been described as the most impressive town entrance in the country. It began in around 1180 as a simple Norman stone tower over a gateway but over the years drum towers were added and then an elaborate façade with battlements. It was designed to protect the town but was also where tolls and taxes were collected.

The south side of the Bargate looks very different and was much restored in the nineteenth century. On the first floor is the Guildhall, used by the burgesses (important merchants) as a meeting place and courtroom. There is a statue of George III dressed as a Roman emperor, a sundial and a curfew bell.

When the Walls of Southampton completely surrounded the town, there were 29 towers and 7 gates. Unfortunately there are now large gaps in the circuit, particularly on the eastern side. What remains is still probably the most impressive and certainly the highest town wall in England with a variety of construction styles. The northern walls, stretching from Polymond Tower to Arundel Tower and including the Bargate, were the first to be built. The last part of the walls to be completed were the arcades in 1380.

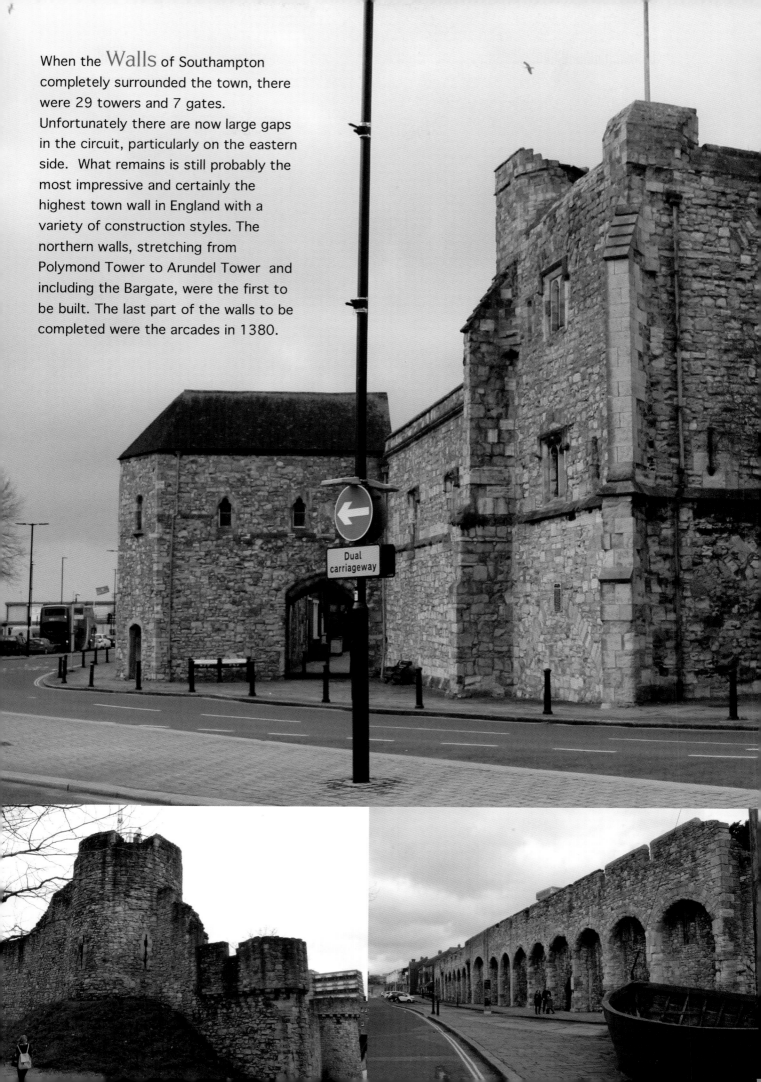

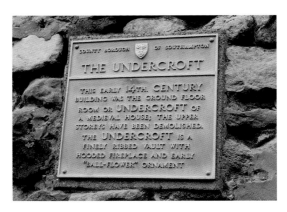

There are hundreds of medieval
Vaults underneath the old town of
Southampton. Some of them are cellars
of private houses (often of later build),
some are inaccessible for various
reasons and some, perhaps, remain
undiscovered. A few can be visited on
guided walks like those run by
SEE Southampton. Most of them would
have been used for storage particularly
of wine which was a staple of
Southampton's trade. During WW2 they
came into their own as air raid shelters.

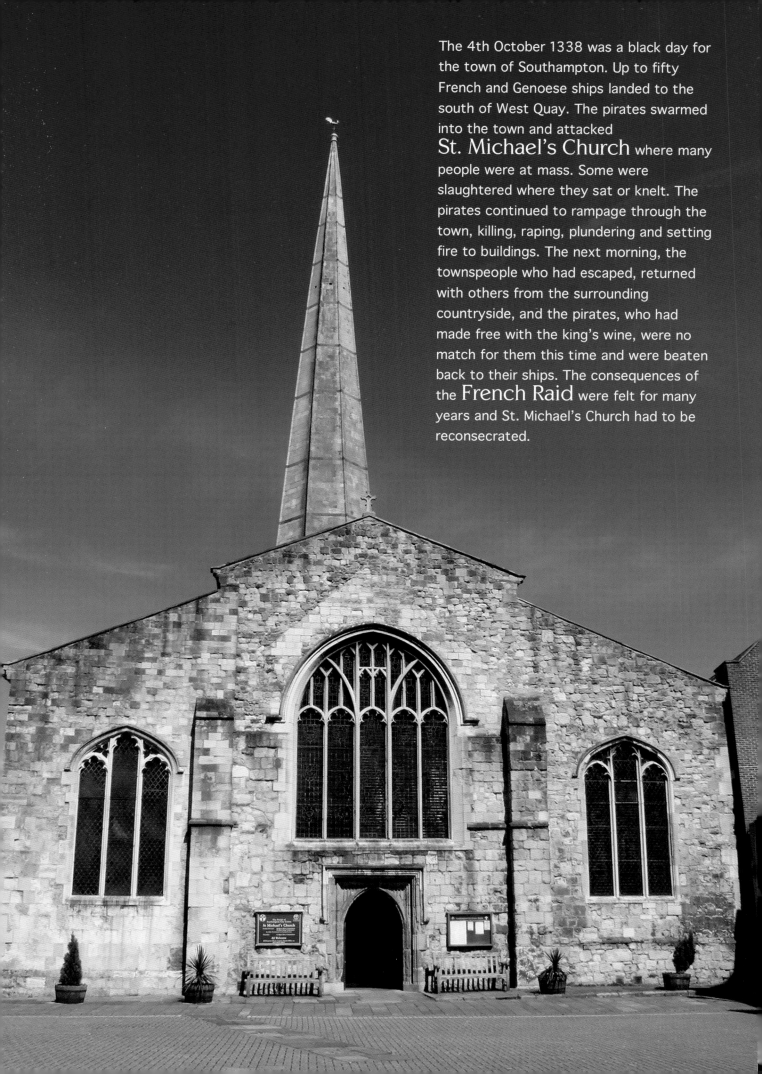

The 4th October 1338 was a black day for the town of Southampton. Up to fifty French and Genoese ships landed to the south of West Quay. The pirates swarmed into the town and attacked

St. Michael's Church

where many people were at mass. Some were slaughtered where they sat or knelt. The pirates continued to rampage through the town, killing, raping, plundering and setting fire to buildings. The next morning, the townspeople who had escaped, returned with others from the surrounding countryside, and the pirates, who had made free with the king's wine, were no match for them this time and were beaten back to their ships. The consequences of the French Raid were felt for many years and St. Michael's Church had to be reconsecrated.

In Memory of
**CAPTAIN
CHARLES ALGERNON FRYATT**
He was born in Southampton 2 December 1871
and died at Bruges on 27 July 1916
during the Great War 1914 - 18

His body was later repatriated and is buried
at Dovercourt, Essex.

He was a ship's captain for the Great Eastern Railway's
passenger and freight steamers and latterly, Master of the
company's vessel SS Brussels.
This plaque was placed here to mark
the centenary of his death.

Holy Rood, which dates from Saxon times, was always regarded as the 'Sailor's Church' It was hit by an incendiary bomb during the Southampton Blitz on the night of 30th November 1940. Eyewitnesses described the church being consumed by flames and recalled the eerie sound of the bells ringing because of the effects of the heat. When December 1st dawned, Holy Rood was a smoking, blackened ruin. As early as 1946 the proposal was put forward that the church should be preserved as a ruin and dedicated to those in the Merchant Navy who lost their lives at sea. The memorials inside the ruin include the Titanic Crew Memorial.

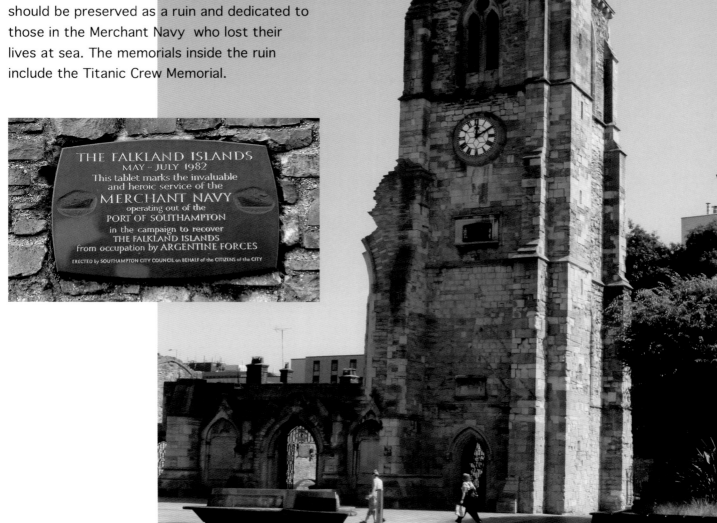

THE FALKLAND ISLANDS
MAY - JULY 1982
This tablet marks the invaluable
and heroic service of the
MERCHANT NAVY
operating out of the
PORT OF SOUTHAMPTON
in the campaign to recover
THE FALKLAND ISLANDS
from occupation by ARGENTINE FORCES

ERECTED by SOUTHAMPTON CITY COUNCIL on BEHALF of the CITIZENS of the CITY

Henry V arrived in Southampton in
July 1415 with his mind set on war with
France. Before he could leave, he had to deal
with a plot revealed to him by his cousin, the
Earl of March, who was keen to save his own
head. The Earl of Cambridge, Lord Scrope
and Sir Thomas Grey were plotting to replace
Henry with his cousin, who also had a strong
claim to the throne. A trial took place and
the three conspirators were all executed in
front of the Bargate.

On the 11th August, Henry passed through
the Westgate to join a flotilla only
surpassed by the size of that gathered for
D-Day. He set off for victory at Agincourt.
Other important departures through the
Westgate, include Edward III and his long
bowmen, heading for victory at Crécy in 1346
and the Pilgrim Fathers heading for a new life
in America in 1620.

Model belonging to Geoffrey Wheeler

On 29th July 1620 The Mayflower arrived in Southampton Water. A week later the Speedwell tied up at West Quay carrying a number of English religious separatists who had been living for some time in Holland. They were to become known as the Pilgrim Fathers.

They planned to spend three days in the port, buying all the supplies that would be needed for the Atlantic crossing and the setting up of their new lives in the New World. The Speedwell was found to be leaking and so their departure date was delayed for another week. When they finally left Southampton on 15th August, it was planned to be their final goodbye to England but the problems with the Speedwell led to further disruptions to their Journey.

GARRET & HAYSOM
MASONS

For a short time Southampton enjoyed popularity as a Spa Town. A visit by Frederick, Prince of Wales in 1750, after which he praised the experience of bathing in Southampton's waters, boosted the reputation of the town.

Many visitors followed, one of whom was a woman who was to be later regarded as one of England's finest novelists. Jane Austen, while staying with relatives, celebrated her 18th birthday at a dance at The Dolphin Hotel. She later lived at her brother's house in Castle Square from 1806-9.

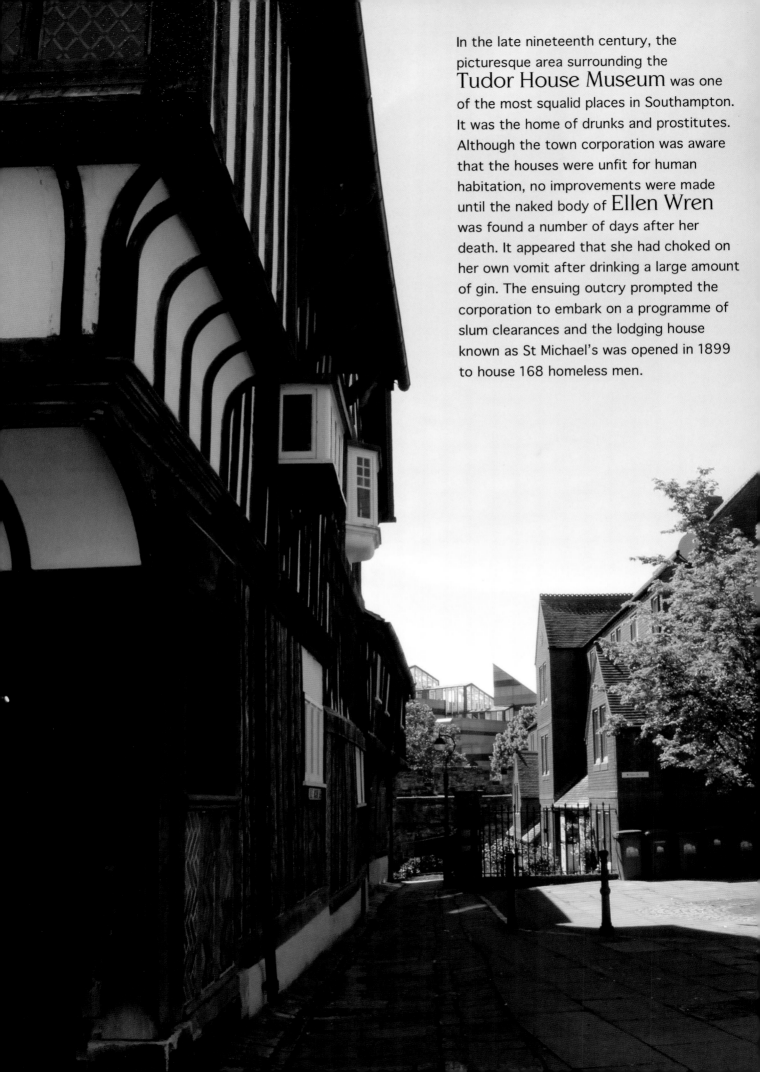

In the late nineteenth century, the picturesque area surrounding the **Tudor House Museum** was one of the most squalid places in Southampton. It was the home of drunks and prostitutes. Although the town corporation was aware that the houses were unfit for human habitation, no improvements were made until the naked body of **Ellen Wren** was found a number of days after her death. It appeared that she had choked on her own vomit after drinking a large amount of gin. The ensuing outcry prompted the corporation to embark on a programme of slum clearances and the lodging house known as St Michael's was opened in 1899 to house 168 homeless men.

Southampton Old Cemetery

is Grade II listed and one of the first municipal cemeteries in the U.K.

The Friends of Southampton Old Cemetery (FoSOC) was founded in 2003 by John Avery, Veronica Tippetts and Geoff Watts. Now it's an enthusiastic voluntary group interested in sharing and preserving the 27 acres of 19th and 20th century graves along with the flora and fauna.

To achieve this care and maintenance, FoSOC holds regular work days which enable the visitors to appreciate the cemetery.

FoSOC can advise and assist in helping relatives research and locate their family graves. Guided walks can also be arranged.

Contact– fosoc1846@googlemail.com

Residents of Southampton are lucky to have large, open green space close to the centre of the city. The 365 acres of The Common feature woodland, heath, lakes and parkland. These habitats support a variety of wildlife, including the rare greater crested newt, and in 1988 the Common was named as a Site of Special Scientific Interest. Notable sites are the Hawthorns Urban Wildlife Centre, a play area for children which was officially opened by ex-Saints player, Frances Benali, in 2018 and the historic local landmark, The Cowherds Inn.

Southampton's Central Parks

were originally the town's fields on which the townspeople grew their crops in summer and grazed their beasts in winter. They were known as Lammas Lands because the crops had to be harvested by Lammas Day (August 1st). Under the 1844 Marsh Act these lands were agreed to be kept as open public spaces for the inhabitants of the town in return for the draining of the Saltmarsh (common land to the south-east) and its commercial development.

RMS Titanic by George A. Fraser

When RMS Titanic sailed away from Southampton on 10th April 1912, everyone knew that not only was she the largest ship in the world at the time but also that she was unsinkable. Four days later she hit an iceberg in the north Atlantic and sank in the early hours of the 15th April with great loss of life. It was a devastating tragedy for the people of Southampton. About 724 crew members came from the town of which only 175 were saved. So many families lost one or more members and these were usually the main earners in the household.

During World War 1 thousands of troops were encamped on Southampton Common awaiting embarkation for France and the trenches. The sight of columns of troops marching down the Avenue, past their church, prompted the parishioners of the

Avenue Congregational Church

to offer help and comfort. From 1914 – 18 they provided hot meals, cigarettes and stationery donated by local businesses; laundry and mending services; posted a multitude of letters and made their hall available for entertainment and leisure. The church was acknowledged at the highest levels after the war for its contribution - including a letter from George V.

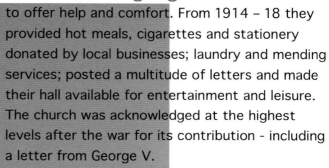

By the 1930s the administration was spread around offices in all parts of the town and it had been clear for a long time that a centralised location was needed. The Civic Centre (the first building to be so named in the country) was the vision of Alderman Sidney Kimber and he planned a building that would house the civic offices, law courts, art gallery and library. He saw it through, with great determination, in the face of much opposition.

Saints' finest moment was when they won the FA cup in 1976, beating Manchester United 1-0. Since then they've had their ups and downs, but the red and white stripes are always a source of pride to the city.

THIS PLAQUE RECORDS THE PURPOSE FULFILLED
BY THIS WORKS IN THE WORLD WAR 1939–1945

UNDER THE STRINGENT SECURITY REQUIREMENTS IMPOSED UPON
US, WE HAD TO CEASE NORMAL ACTIVITY AND CLOSE OUR DOORS
TO OUR CUSTOMERS, HOWEVER IMPORTANT THEIR INDIVIDUAL
WORK. THE WAR WORK CARRIED ON IN THESE PREMISES
TRANSCENDED ALL OTHER PRIORITIES.
WHILST BEING PRIVILEGED BY THE MINISTRY OF AIRCRAFT
PRODUCTION TO RETAIN FULL AND COMPLETE CONTROL OF
OUR WORKS PLANT AND STAFF: WE WERE ADJUDGED SUITABLE
TO UNDERTAKE A COMPREHENSIVE SCHEDULE OF MANUFACTURE
ASSEMBLY AND REPAIR OF MANY FIGHTER AND BOMBER AIRCRAFT
COMPONENTS – SPITFIRE TANKS AND BOMB RELEASE GEAR AND
SEAFIRE ARRESTER GEAR WERE AMONG THE COMPONENTS
MANUFACTURED HERE ~ UNDER THE DIRECTION OF OUR OWN
KEY PERSONNEL, AND BY WADHAM TRAINED WAR WORKERS, OVER
600 OF WHOM WERE EMPLOYED.

The Spitfire, iconic fighter plane of WW2, was developed at the Supermarine factory in Southampton by R.J. Mitchell. He lived just long enough to see the test flights of his creation in 1937. The aircraft was so successful that the aviation works became a prime target for German bombers. A series of attacks in September 1940 eventually saw the total destruction of the factory but plans for the dispersal of the manufacturing process had already started. The often small engineering works all over the town, and elsewhere, ensured the continued building of the fighter plane. They were to become known as 'shadow factories'.

K 5054